BEAUtyshOp fOr the SOUls Of OUr ChIldrEn

My Color Fits Me Like A Glove

Jo Ann Buckner

BALBOA.
PRESS
A DIVISION OF HAY HOUSE

Balboa Press books may be ordered through booksellers or by contacting:

Balboa Press
A Division of Hay House
1663 Liberty Drive
Bloomington, IN 47403
www.balboapress.com
1 (877) 407-4847

Because of the dynamic nature of the Internet, any web addresses or links contained in this book may have changed since publication and may no longer be valid. The views expressed in this work are solely those of the author and do not necessarily reflect the views of the publisher, and the publisher hereby disclaims any responsibility for them.

The author of this book does not dispense medical advice or prescribe the use of any technique as a form of treatment for physical, emotional, or medical problems without the advice of a physician, either directly or indirectly. The intent of the author is only to offer information of a general nature to help you in your quest for emotional and spiritual well-being. In the event you use any of the information in this book for yourself, which is your constitutional right, the author and the publisher assume no responsibility for your actions.

Any people depicted in stock imagery provided by Thinkstock are models, and such images are being used for illustrative purposes only. Certain stock imagery © Thinkstock.

Print information available on the last page.

ISBN: 978-1-5043-7369-2 (sc)
ISBN: 978-1-5043-7370-8 (e)

Balboa Press rev. date: 03/28/2017

BEAUtyshOp fOr thE SOUls Of OUr ChIldrEn

COntEnts

DEdICAtIOn

To the Rainbow Coalition of children around the world. Always remember and appreciate your own unique color and skin complexion... It fits you like a glove... God chose it especially for you, then painted you with love!

To Jazz.To quote from my own song: "There's a song in my soul that sings you are whole. Everywhere I go.. It sings, You Are Whole." Thank you and your hubby, Chaka, so much for your whole-hearted support. Love and Blessings to you!

To my nephew "K.P." whose experience of discrimination in the classroom of life made this book possible. To my grandchildren Anthony, Angela, Natasha and Lewayne. To all my young nieces and nephews; Always remember.. God chose your color, Then painted you with love. *Wear it Proud!*

BAckgrOUnd

In his kindergarten class my nephew K.P. was introduced to the harsh reality of racism. K.P. was the only African descent child in an otherwise all white class. None of his classmates reflected back in the special color which God had painted him. Still, they became friends. Then one day his classroom buddy had a birthday. To celebrate the occasion, the child's mother planned a party, brought invitations to the classroom, then distributed the invitations to every child in the classroom except K.P. He was deeply, profoundly confused, and devastated by the experience. However his young friend removed all doubt and mystery. He told him, "you didn't get an invitation because my mother said that Black people can not come to her house."

COntEnt

Content means what's inside of something or someone. What's inside of the jar? Discuss what is inside of each jar.

Have each child imagine what is inside of Jar #3. Discuss with each one what he/she imagined. Explain the relationship between the imaginations of each child/ children and their inability to determine the unknown contents of Jar #3. The teacher or facilitator will fill the jar with various items (unseen by the child), e.g., rocks, spices, needles, erasers, etc.

Explain the impossibility of determining the content of one's character by the color of their skin.

_____

_____

_____

_____

_____

_____

_____

_____

_____

_____

_____

_____

_____

_____

_____

_____

_____

_____

CHArACtEr

Character is the combination of things inside of something or someone... like you when you combine sugar, water and Kool- Aide to make a drink. Or your mommy may combine water in a pot with coffee grounds to make coffee. So " character" is the combination of what's inside of you, how you think, feel, believe and behave.

When someone is afraid of everything like cats, dogs, frogs and strangers, you might call him a "scaredy cat." His character would be "scary." Or when someone is always polite, kind and always nice to everyone, children and adults, his character would be "kind."

Although we are born with a certain kind of character, we can improve our behavior or unlearn unwanted behavior to develop our character.

CHARACTERISTICS

Characteristics are the traits which determine your behavior. Which of the following characteristic are yours?

- happy
- thoughtful
- clever
- funny
- obedient
- silly
- selfish
- kind
- respectful

Your own characteristics are what makes you different from others. If the word that best suits you is not listed, add that word to the list.

VOCABULARY

Ask your mommy, daddy or teacher to help you with the meaning of any words that you do not know or understand. Those words then become a part of your vocabulary.

"Vocabulary" is the combination of all words you know. For example, if you know the following words: dog, cat, rat, run stop, learn, candy, mom, sister, teacher, polite, school, party.

How many words would there be in your vocabulary?

"Do not wish to be anything but what you are, and try to be that perfectly." St. Francis de Sales

Martin Luther King Jr. had a dream. He said that he hoped that:

"One day his children would grow up to be judged by the content of their character and not the color of their skin."

What is the content of your character? Do other people like your character? Option: Describe the content of your character. Make up a story about your character. Tell why someone/anyone would like your character.

_____

_____

_____

_____

_____

_____

_____

_____

_____

_____

_____

_____

_____

_____

_____

_____

_____

_____

_____

_____

_____

_____

_____

_____

_____

What Can You Do To Develop A Better Character?

What can you do to develop a character of:

- appreciation
- honesty
- kindness
- intelligence
- obedience
- imagination

Have children think of a task he/she can do that will help to develop any of the above characteristics.

Example: I could develop the character of "honesty" if I always tell the truth about myself and others.

_____

_____

_____

_____

_____

_____

_____

_____

_____

_____

Character Faces

Fill in the blank with the word you think fits best.

When someone does or says something that makes you feel good you have a _____ face.

When someone does or says something that hurts your feelings you have a _____ face.

Tell a story about a time you felt like one of these facial expressions.

CrEAtE a ChArActEr

Make up a story about your character.

What is your character's name? How many sisters and brothers does he/she have? What is his/her favorite food, game, toy, place, color? Who is his/her favorite person? How big is your character? How old is your character? Does he/she have a nickname?

_____

_____

_____

_____

_____

_____

_____

_____

_____

_____

_____

_____

_____

_____

_____

_____

_____

_____

_____

What is the Content of Your Character?

Choose the content of a friend's character from the list below.

- happy
- shy
- silly
- kind
- thoughtful
- funny
- smart
- sad
- bully
- fearful

If the desired words are not listed you can get a blank card and write on it the word of your choice. Now take the card and place it anywhere on your friend's body.

Special note: Whatever characteristic you have chosen applies to you and your friend. For we only see ourselves in others and we are drawn to those who see themselves in us.

Discuss the difference between you and your chosen friend. Now discuss how are you the same even though your faces and skin color may be different?

Storytelling: Tell a story about your friendship.

Explain to the child/children that even though the faces of their friends may be of a different color, the content of their character can be the same.

Discuss that "character" is the result of a combination of traits (honesty, happy, clever) and not the result of the color of one's skin.

_____

_____

_____

_____

_____

_____

_____

_____

_____

_____

_____

"MY COLOR FITS ME LIKE A GLOVE"

My color fits me like a glove,

God chose it for me

Then painted me with Love

Radiant

Vibrant!

Sweet as berries on a vine.

I hope you love your color,

As much as I love mine.

Have child/children create a second verse for the above poem using the following phrase:

My color fits me like a glove because...

"We may not always be able to build a future for our youth. But we can always build our youth for the future."-President Franklin D. Roosevelt

Character Building Activities

1. Greetings
   Back during the time when I was a child, greetings were a common courtesy. It was compulsory for children to demonstrate respect by greeting others as they came into their presence. To greet anyone is to acknowledge them as a human being. *"Let's bring common courtesy back to the future as we strengthen the content of our character."* Discuss with the children how it feels when others act as if they do not exist by seeing them and not greeting them.

2. What I like best about me
   Discuss with the children the importance of recognizing the best in self, as well as others. Have children list their best traits and/or skills.

   Often when children are hurt or embarrassed publicly their creativity shuts down. The writing here is to encourage their creativity.

   _____

   _____

   _____

   _____

   _____

   _____

   _____

   _____

   _____

   _____

   _____

   _____

3. "It takes an entire village to raise a child" *African proverb*
   The facilitator discusses with the children what an African village looks like. This activity helps the children to understand how everyone they meet could have an effect on their lives. Describe what the "African village houses" look like….. what materials are thy made of.. Activities that go on in a village: Mothers often sell food on the roads to raise money. Animals are often seen in the village: goats, chickens and other farm animals. Mothers carry the infants and toddlers on their backs while working. Usually there are no lights in the villages nor running water.. they use well water. They carry the water container on their heads. Compare a city neighborhood to village life… people, places and things you see in a neighborhood. After the discussion the participants get to create a village.. using and reinforcing their creativity. Items needed to create the village: Paper plates, crayons, paint, large paper bags, glue, other crafts. They can do art work.. be creative. They then tell the story of the village using their creation. Note: Participants can present in play form the village life… to family, friends or the classroom. Discuss what they learned with them.

_____

_____

_____

_____

_____

_____

_____

_____

_____

_____

African Village

HEArt art

The HEART has an EAR to HEAR. That's why the word HEART contains the word HEAR and the word HEAR contains the word EAR. The word HEART contains the word ART. There is an ART to listening with the HEART. EVERYONE must do their own PART of the ART. Let's start here… lend me your EAR. Together we'll make a new EARTH.

By Jo Ann Buckner

Participant Activity: Participants will engage in an activity to develop active listening with the heart. They are instructed to pay attention to the ideas and thoughts that come into their heads..before taking any action.. take a deep breath..Use your thinking cap… Imagine it on your head.. then "send" that thought or word or action image straight to your heart center. Ask the question: Does this make my heart feel good? Notice how you feel… good, bad, mad or sad? If it makes your heart feel happy..do it! If not.. then do not do it. Give yourself a high five .. your heart is alive! You are now practicing Heart Art.

_____

_____

_____

_____

_____

_____

_____

_____

_____

_____

_____

_____

_____

_____

_____

_____

_____

_____

After completing the prior activity, the participants will have a far greater understanding of themselves and others than they had before because they have learned to listen to their heart. By learning to listen to your heart you are able to create a new earth. The H in heart is shifted from before the E to after the T, creating a new earth.

aftErwOrd

In view of the recent spotlight coverage on television, radio and the internet regarding race relations, it appears that this is an ideal time to reach out to our youngsters to assist them in building self-esteem. As Dr. Martin Luther King Jr. said, "A man should be judged by the content of his character rather than the color and complexion of his skin." I agree.

Even though it has been decades now since he spoke those words, the evidence of the need to live up to those standards is still present. Consequently, I strongly believe that a workbook - which I self-published and used 20 years ago - is very much a viable vehicle that will empower our children with this concept. Therefore, I have decided to republish the workbook. Since seeds of inequality are often sown at an early age, such as in kindergarten, it would behoove us to begin training at that level.

"My Color Fits Me Like A Glove" was born as a result of a painful and shameful experience that occurred in a public school kindergarten class. Not only must those who are recipients of such insensitivity be addressed, it must necessarily include other youngsters who witness such encounters.

about the author

Jo Ann Buckner, RSCp. MA Counseling

A former US Peace Corps Volunteer, she has also served as a teacher, counselor, workshop facilitator, and storyteller who spent two years in West Africa. She is a Licensed Practitioner. She has traveled on five continents and 47 states. She is a mother and grandmother. Jo Ann hails from Indianapolis, Indiana and currently lives in Las Vegas, Nevada.

epilogue

Beauty Shop for the Souls of Our Children is a program of personal and professional transformation that was given to Jo Ann Buckner during meditation. Beauty Shop For The Soul of our Children addresses the fact that we are multi-dimensional beings in a physical form. However, a major aspect of our being is mental and emotional. In recent decades, we are becoming more enlightened and empowered with increased awareness and understanding of the impact of our emotions and our thoughts upon our physical bodies. Scientists tell us that the mental and emotional imprints upon our psyches begin as early as in the womb and continue with us on the tomb.

For more information about Beauty Shop For The Soul of Our Children contact:

ourbeautifulsouls123@gmail.com